Negative Calorie Diet

Lose 10 pounds in 10 days with delicious healthy recipes

Cookbook for rapid fat loss without starving

By: Albert Pino

Table of Contents

Legal notice

Join Albert Pino's VIP Club

Get access to exclusive content from Albert including healthy living tips, tricks and hacks, special discounts, recipes, and free books!

www.albertpino.com

Negative Calorie Diet

Introduction

The Negative Calorie Diet is a fairly new diet regimen that is presently taking the world by storm. The basic concept behind the negative calorie diet is not to consume foods that contain negative calories. This is impossible. All food contains calories that your body burns for energy. Not all foods contain the same number of calories, of course. Foods like celery and kale are very low in calories while foods like meat, especially fatty meat, have very high calorie counts.

So how is it possible to eat a negative calorie diet if all foods contain calories? The answer is that the body must use energy in the process of eating, digestion, and waste elimination. The body burns calories throughout this process and this caloric expenditure is what opens up the possibility of consuming foods that have a net negative caloric value. This means that although the foods themselves contain calories, the total number of calories the food contains is less than the number of calories required to eat, digest, and eliminate that food.

.

Chapter 1: What Is a Negative Calorie Diet?

Negative calorie foods all have a few things in common. Perhaps the most important is a high concentration of water within the food. This is important because water contains 0 calories and the body must burn 1 calorie per ounce of water consumed. This means that the greater your water consumption, the more calories you will burn. For this reason, foods with significant water content will often be negative calorie foods.

Another important quality is the fiber content in food. Fiber is not digested by the body but rather it simply passes through the body. According to research, around 5 to 10% of a person's total energy expenditure for a day is dedicated to eliminating fiber from the body, and in turn, work on storing the nutrients taken from it, and turning it into energy that the body can use. Certain vegetables, celery for example, contain very high levels of fiber. For this reason, the negative calorie diet depends largely on the consumption of fresh vegetables.

In addition to a high water and fiber content, the negative calorie diet eschews processed foods, opting instead to include unprocessed, natural whole foods. That is, foods that appear on your plate essentially as they would appear in nature. When food is processed it is typically treated with a variety of chemicals meant to enhance taste and artificially extend its shelf life . Neither of these goals have your health in mind, but rather they are the objectives of a profit seeking corporation seeking to maximize it's own bottom line, rather than seeking to maximize your health and wellness. You want to avoid processed foods while on a negative calorie diet.

What you end up with when you take all of the above factors into account is a group of negative calorie foods that include things like cruciferous vegetables, leafy green vegetables, celery, and edible nightshades.

For those who are unaware, nightshades is a family of foods that includes eggplant, chilies, tomatoes, peppers, and several other foods. Be aware that these foods can be harmful to people with autoimmune disorders. For those that do not have such disorders however, these are healthy foods.

When it comes to protein, we're looking to include small portions of lean meat and muscle fibers that will enhance your metabolic function without putting you into positive calorie territory. The recipes in this book will ensure you don't end up blowing your negative calorie diet by over-consuming meat. Just make sure you always favor lean rather than fatty cuts.

Negative Calorie Diet

Chapter 2: How The Negative Calorie Diet Can Help You Lose Weight

Here's the thing: the more negative calorie foods you eat, the more weight you lose. When you consume negative calorie foods, it means that the process of consuming and digesting the foods causes your body to use more energy (more calories) than is contained in the food. This creates a caloric deficit which in turn causes your body to turn to it's stored fat reserves as a source of energy. Essentially, you are forcing your body to burn up your stored fat cells!

You see, your overall calorie intake will ultimately be reduced when you eat negative calorie foods instead of high calorie ones—and if you exercise as you do so, you will really see a substantial amount of weight loss.

It is crucial to note that while you are following the negative calorie diet, you must avoid eating sugar or highly processed foods. If you insist on making an exception to the no sugar rule, you should use Stevia as opposed to sugar or a chemically processed artificial sweetener. It's also important not to use any artificial, commercially produced dressings because more often than not, they contain significant quantities of sugar.

Negative Calorie Diet

Chapter 3: What Are Cruciferous Vegetables and Why They Are an Important Part of a Negative Calorie Diet?

Cruciferous vegetables are an important part of the Negative Calorie Diet.

Cruciferous vegetables come from the Cruciferae Family. The name originated from "Cruciferae", which in early Latin literally means "cross-bearing", an allusion to the shape of the flowers that seem to resemble crosses. Prime examples of cruciferous vegetables include: *Brussels sprouts, bok choy, garden cress, broccoli, cabbage,* and *cauliflower.*

These vegetables are known to be essential parts of the Negative Calorie Diet because they are high in cellulose, water, and vitamin C, together with essential phytochemicals and nutrients that the body needs.

Most cruciferous vegetables also contain glucosinolates that are said to prevent cancer, drive toxins away from the body, and could suit the taste of many—and that's why they are used in most plant-based recipes.

But most importantly, cruciferous vegetables are nutritionally dense foods. This means they pack lots of nutrients, vitamins, and minerals that promote good health in to very few calories. By consuming cruciferous vegetables you can easily ensure you get a full day's supply of nutrients without eating excessive calories. Indeed, when on the

Negative Calorie Diet it is impossible to consume excess calories. You can eat as much as you want because the foods you are eating only deepen the caloric deficit, promoting further weight loss!

Chapter 4: What Are the Most Important Foods in a Negative Calorie Diet?

In this chapter, you'll learn about the most important foods that should be part of a Negative Calorie Diet. Check them out below:

Arugula

Arugula contains only 4 calories per cup.

Aside from being low in calories, it's also low in cholesterol and fat—which most health-conscious people don't want in their diets, too. On the other hand, it is high in potassium, Vitamins C, K, and A, fiber, and other important nutrients. Arugula is also filled with antioxidants that drive toxins away —and kill free radicals that damage the body.

Asparagus

Asparagus contains 27 calories per cup.

It is known as one of the most traditional detoxifying foods because it's able to act as a diuretic that drives toxins away and speeds up metabolism in the body. It also contains important vitamins and minerals, such as protein, copper, iron, folate, and Vitamins B6, K, E, C, and A, among others.

Broccoli

Broccoli contains 31 calories per cup.

Broccoli is known as a great superfood because it's filled with mostly everything you need: antioxidants, minerals, vitamins, and even fiber that not only help you lose weight, but also help prevent various diseases, such as cancer!

Broth

Clear broth of seafood, chicken, beef, or miso contains only 10 calories per cup.

What's great about broth is that it works like a kind of "secret weapon" because it makes you feel satiated without making you fat. It nourishes your body thoroughly—and that's why it is important that you make use of it.

Brussels Sprouts

This contains 38 calories per cup.

What's great about Brussels sprouts is that they're loaded with fiber and phytonutrients that make you lose weight and that prevent cancer. Some people may not like the taste of them at first, but when cooked right, they actually taste amazing.

Cabbage

Cabbage contains 22 calories per cup.

Cabbage contains anti-carcinogenic properties as well as anti-fat properties, such as glucosinolate, phytonutrients, and other vitamins and minerals. It's also easy to use cabbage in a lot of recipes, which makes it a staple food of the Negative Calorie Diet. If you aren't already, you should try to consume more purple cabbage as it has a lot of natural chemicals and anthocyanins.

Lettuce
Lettuce contains only 5 calories per cup.

Aside from an extremely low amount of calories, what you can expect about lettuce is that no matter how much you eat of it, it still won't make you gain a lot of weight. Lettuce that contains the most nutrients are red leaf, purple, or dark green.

Beets
Beets contain 37 calories per cup.

What's amazing about beets is that although they are sweet, they actually do not contain sugar and they are also filled with fiber, antioxidants, potassium, folate, and iron!

Cauliflower
Cauliflower contains 25 calories per cup.

Cauliflower is a great source of folate. It's also filled with lots of Vitamin C and phytonutrients that help you lose weight, and prevent the formation of cancer. It's also a good rice substitute, and is one of the most important superfoods around.

Coffee
Coffee contains zero calories.

What's great about coffee is that when you take it in moderation, you can experience surprising health benefits. Coffee is able to alter the amount of peptides in the body—or those hormones that are released to say you are satiated. It makes you feel that you are full already. It has also been linked to reduced rates of Parkinson's and liver cancer.

Grapefruit

Grapefruit contains 39 calories per half a fruit.

Grapefruit is part of many diets and is a popular food to eat when doing a Negative Calorie Diet. It has high nutrient content and a low calorie count. It also contains soluble fibers, potassium, folic acid and Vitamin C that could prevent atherosclerosis. Choose red and pink varieties for maximum effect.

Mushrooms

Mushrooms contain 15 calories per cup.

Mushrooms are not just the favorite pizza toppings of some, they're also very healthy. Mushrooms can boost and protect the immune system as they contain fiber, B Vitamins, potassium, and loads of antioxidants! The best variants include Portobello, Shitake, and White, although other varieties are also great.

Tomatoes

Tomatoes contain 22 calories per cup.

Tomatoes contain lots of antioxidants and lycopene that protect your skin against cancer and the harsh UV rays of the sun. Tomatoes also have high amounts of vitamin C, fiber, and potassium, as well.

Turnips

Turnips contain 36 calories per cup.

Turnips promise low glycemic index, which means you'll also be protected from diabetes, and is also one of the best sources of vitamin C.

Watercress

Watercress contains only 4 calories per cup.

As its name suggests, this one is really filled with cellulose and water and has cancer-fighting, detoxifying properties. It also protects you against other diseases because it contains sulforaphane and other compounds that lower the risk of getting afflicted with all these various diseases.

Zucchini

Zucchini contains 20 calories per cup.

Another favorite, zucchini is sometimes known as the "miracle squash" because it allows you to feel satiated— without filling you up with calories. It's also filled with Vitamin A!

Spinach

Spinach contains only 7 calories per cup.

Another miraculous vegetable, spinach is quite flavorful. It contains Vitamin K, Folic Acid, iron, beta-carotene, and phytonutrients that help you lose weight and protect you against loads of diseases. It also prevents macular degeneration.

Lemon and Lime

These contain 20 calories per fruit.

These are both rich in vitamin C and are some of the best sources of fiber. They also protect you against common illnesses, and improve your respiratory system, as well.

Kale

Kale contains 5 calories per cup.

In recent years Kale has rightfully taken its place as a favorite superfood for health and weight loss. Kale can help protect against breast cancer and certain other cancers and is also filled with lots of phytonutrients. Aside from that, it's also one of the best sources of manganese, folic acid, and many vitamins.

Garlic

Garlic contains 4 calories per clove.

Garlic is amazing because it strengthens the immune system and helps fight colds, together with most urinary infections. It has lots of antimicrobial and antiviral properties!

Pepper

Peppers contain 30 calories per cup.

These contain capsaicin that satiate the body and easily burns fat, and also has good amounts of vitamin C fiber that can propel the body even more.

Onions

Onions contain 32 calories per cup.

Aside from being flavorful, onions also contain sulfides that protect the body against many forms of cancer, especially endometrial ones.

Pumpkin

Pumpkin contains 30 calories per cup.

Pumpkin has many antioxidants, beta-carotene, and essential vitamins. It's also so easy to add to a lot of dishes, so it's a great part of any diet! It lowers blood pressure, as well.

Radish

Radishes contain 19 calories per cup.

They aid in digestion because they contain lots of sulfur compounds, antioxidants, and folic acid, and has twice the amount of calcium that leafy vegetables have!

Tea

Tea contains no calories, just like coffee.

But of course, tea could be considered as the healthier version—especially when you take green, oolong, white, or black. It lessens the amount of bad cholesterol in the body, and also protects you against osteoporosis and cancer! Doing a 7 day tea cleanse is another great way to detox, re-energize, and lose weight. If you are interested in learning more about how tea cleansing works, check out my best-selling book: 7 Day Tea Cleanse by Albert Pino, available on Amazon.

Fennel

Fennel contains 27 calories per cup.

This prevents winter coughs, boosts your immune system, and is filled with lots of vitamins and minerals, as well!

Celery

Celery contains 16 calories per cup.

What's great about celery is that it's filled with cellulose and it's known as one of the most effective negative calorie foods. You can eat an unlimited amount of celery and you won't get fat. Celery is also perfect for those who are trying to have healthy pregnancies, and is also filled with folate, Vitamin C, and vitamin A, amongst others. The only caution about celery is that the porous stalks are known to be hard to fully clean of pesticides. For this reason, it is strongly recommended that you purchase only organic celery.

Carrots

Carrots contain 22 calories per half a cup.

They are so low in cholesterol and fat, which makes them a perfect part of this diet. They're also rich in beta-carotene and vitamin A—essential nutrients that the body needs.

Chapter 5: Negative Calorie Diet Recipes

Veggie-stuffed Mushrooms

Ingredients:

¼ cup fresh chives, chopped

1/3 cup kalamata olives, chopped

1 ½ cups tomatoes, chopped

½ tsp freshly ground black pepper

¼ tsp coarse salt

1 ½ tsp balsamic vinegar

2 tsp olive oil

4 large Portobello mushroom cups

Instructions:

First, preheat the oven to 400 F.

Arrange the mushroom caps with gill-sides up on a baking sheet. Drizzle the mushrooms with vinegar and oil, and season with salt and pepper. Bake for around 10 minutes or just until tender.

Mix tomatoes, chives, and olives in a bowl. Season with ¼ tsp pepper.

Divide the mixture over the mushrooms and bake for 10 to 12 minutes more, or just until tender.

Serve and enjoy!

Asparagus and Beet Salad with Honey Lemon Vinaigrette

Ingredients:

1 tsp ground black pepper

1 tsp iodized salt

2 Tbsp Extra Virgin Olive Oil

2 lbs asparagus, trimmed and cut into ¾ inch pieces

2 15 oz cans sliced beets, drained and diced

For the Vinaigrette:

½ cup extra virgin olive oil

½ tsp ground black pepper

½ tsp iodized salt

2 Tbsp honey

1 Tbsp white vinegar

1 orange, zested, 2 Tbsp juice reserved

1 lemon zested, 2 Tbsp juice reserved

1 Tbsp onion, chopped

Instructions:

First, preheat the oven to 375 F.

Combine oil, asparagus, pepper, and salt in a bowl. Bake until tender or for 8 to 10 minutes in baking pan. Wait for it to cool.

Combine all the ingredients for the vinaigrette in a blender with the exception of the oil, and puree until smooth.

Add the oil to the vinaigrette slowly while the blender is on medium speed.

Then, combine the beets, asparagus, goat cheese, and vinaigrette in a medium bowl. Toss until well-coated, and season with salt and pepper, to taste.

Braised Carrots and Cabbage

Ingredients:

For the seasoning:

1 Tbsp garlic powder

½ Tbsp lemon powder

1 tsp celery seed

1 tsp cayenne

For the dish:

Salt and freshly ground black pepper

1 bag baby carrots

2 Tbsp seasoning (with ingredients listed above)

1 cup water

1 large green cabbage

Instructions:

First, work on the cabbage by coring it and then chop it into 2-inch pieces. Make sure to clean the cabbage thoroughly before letting it drain.

Next, add the seasoning, water, and cabbage and wait for it to simmer and steam for at least 2 hours. Do stir until carrots are tender, or at least every 15 minutes. Add salt and pepper, to taste.

Serve and enjoy!

Celery and Radicchio Salad

Ingredients:

1 head radicchio, quartered and cored, with leaves separated and torn in half

4 stalks celery

6 scallions, sliced thinly

3 Tbsp flat-leaf parsley, chopped roughly

½ cup extra virgin olive oil

2 anchovy fillets in oil, drained and chopped finely

2 tsp Dijon mustard

½ red onion, chopped finely

¼ cup red wine vinegar

2 cloves garlic, minced

Freshly ground black pepper and kosher salt

1 ½ cups dried cannellini beans, soaked overnight and drained

Instructions:

Combine 6 cups of water with beans in a 4-quart saucepan. Bring to a boil. Then, reduce the heat until the dish simmers. Cook the beans for around 45 minutes—or until tender. Then, drain the beans before transferring to a bowl and begin to season with salt and pepper, to taste.

Use the sides of your knife to smash and press the garlic on a cutting board until it becomes pasty. Then, scrape the said paste onto a bowl and mix with onion and vinegar. Allow the onions to stand for at least 10 minutes before whisking anchovies and mustard in. Drizzle the mixture with olive oil until it emulsifies and then season with salt and pepper, to taste. Reserve at least ¼ cup of the dressing, and then pour over the remaining beans. Coat by tossing.

Toss the dressing that you have reserved in a small bowl with celery, parsley, and scallions, and season with salt and pepper, once more. Arrange the radicchio in a single layer on a serving platter, and then top with the cannellini beans. Spoon the scallions and the celery on top, as well.

Endive and Green Beans Salad

Ingredients:

4 Tbsp parsley, chopped finely

4 Tbsp red onions, chopped finely

4 Tbsp olive oil

2 Tbsp red wine vinegar

2 Tbsp Dijon mustard

2 large Belgian Endives

1 lb fresh green beans

Salt and freshly ground black pepper, to taste

Instructions:

Trim the ends of the green beans off. Cut into 1 to 1 ½ inch lengths. Simmer for 3 to 5 minutes in boiling water. Make sure not to overcook so they would remain tender and crisp. Make sure to drain well and let cool.

Next, trim the ends of the endives off and cut into bite-sized pieces. Rinse in cold water and spin dry.

Next, put pepper, salt, vinegar, and mustard in a bowl, and blend well using wire whisk. Add oil while mixing lightly. Add onions, green beans, endives, and parsley.

Toss the salad well, serve, and enjoy!

Jicama, Orange, and Kale Salad

Ingredients:

1 cup jicama, peeled and cut into matchstick-pieces

1/8 tsp black pepper

¼ tsp garlic powder

1/8 tsp cinnamon

¼ tsp cumin

½ cup + 2 Tbsp raw almonds

1 Tbsp fresh lemon juice

¼ tsp Himalayan sea salt

1 Tbsp + 1 tsp extra virgin olive oil

1 bunch Dinosaur Kale

½ cup raisins

2 large navel oranges

Instructions:

Zest and juice one of the oranges and then add the raisins to the juice before reserving the zest.

Then, remove the kale's stems and reserve—or discard, if you want to. Julienne the leaves and then mix the kale with lemon juice, salt, and olive oil in another bowl. Make sure to use your hands to massage the kale and then break it down and soften it in just 3 minutes.

Whiz ½ cup of the almonds in a food processor or blender. Do so until they have been finely ground, and then chop the rest of the almonds.

Add orange zest to the kale mixture, and then add raisins and juice. Then, add the almonds, cinnamon, cumin, black pepper, garlic powder, and jicama. Toss well to combine.

Peel or section the rest of the orange.

Serve and enjoy!

Roasted Spinach, Onions, and Butternut Squash

Ingredients:

1/3 cup pecans, chopped

1/3 cup dried cranberries, sweetened

3 oz fresh spinach, stems removed and leaves torn in bite-sized pieces

2 Tbsp olive oil

1 cup red onion, chopped

1 butternut squash

Instructions:

Preheat the oven to 450 F after greasing a baking sheet lightly.

Slice the butternut squash into 1 inch pieces crosswise. Make sure to peel and clean each of them and discard stringy pulp, plus remove the seeds.

Then, toss the squash cubes together with olive oil and onion until well-coated in a bowl before transferring to a baking sheet.

Roast until squash is tender or for around 25 to 30 minutes.

Then, toss the squash cubes together with pecans, dried cranberries, and spinach in a bowl.

Serve warm and enjoy!

Sautéed Cherry Tomatoes and Zucchini

Ingredients:

1 Tbsp fresh chopped basil, more for garnish (if desired)

¼ tsp freshly ground black pepper

1 tsp salt

2 cloves garlic, minced

1 pint cherry tomatoes, halved

1 lb zucchini, cut into 1 to 2 inch chunks

1 small red onion, diced

2 Tbsp extra virgin olive oil

Instructions:

First, heat olive oil in a pan over medium heat.

Then, add the onions and stir for at least 7 to 8 minutes or until pale in color and make sure not to let them brown.

Then, add the tomatoes, zucchini, garlic, pepper, and salt, and cook until zucchini is crisp or for around 3 to 5 minutes. Make sure the tomatoes have also collapsed so there would be some sauce.

Add the fresh basil then add seasoning, to taste.

Transfer contents to a serving dish and serve with more basil, if desired.

Turnip and Radish

Ingredients:

1 Tbsp chives, chopped finely

2 Tbsp mint leaves, sliced thinly

Pepper

Salt

¼ cup low-sodium chicken broth

1/3 cup water

1 ½ lb small turnips

1 ½ lb radishes

1 large shallot

2 Tbsp ghee

Instructions:

Melt ghee in a 12-inch skillet in medium-high heat.

Add the shallots and cook until tender and golden, or for at least 2 minutes. Make sure to stir occasionally.

Add turnips and radishes, and stir until well-coated.

Add broth, water, ground black pepper, and salt, and then heat until it boils.

Reduce heat to medium low, and then cover for 15 minutes while cooking.

Take the lid off the saucepan and cook for another 7 to 10 minutes or until the liquid of the vegetables have evaporated, and the vegetables have been properly glazed.

Take the dish away from heat and add chives and mint before placing in a serving platter.

Garnish with mint leaves and serve.

Tomato Garlic Kale Salad

Ingredients:

Five sun-dried tomatoes

A handful of finely chopped kale

A handful of finely chopped spinach

1 Tbsp pumpkin seeds

¼ small, red onion

One garlic clove

For the dressing: 1 tsp apple cider vinegar

1 Tbsp cold pressed oil

A dash of garlic powder, pepper and chili

¼ tsp salt

For the toppings: fresh herbs and cherry tomatoes

Instructions:

Place spinach and kale in a bowl and mix the dressing ingredients in another bowl.

Pour the dressing over the greens then chop the tomatoes, red onion and garlic clove. Add them to the greens and sprinkle pumpkin seeds on top.

Mix until well-combined and serve topped with cherry tomatoes and fresh herbs. Enjoy!

Radish Lettuce Tomato Salad

Ingredients:

2 cups romaine lettuce, washed, dried and torn

1 cup red lettuce, torn

1 cup radicchio, torn

1 cup escarole, torn

½ green bell pepper, sliced into rings

12 cherry tomatoes

½ red bell pepper, sliced into rings

2 Tbsp lemon juice

¼ cup balsamic vinegar

2 Tbsp fresh basil, chopped

¼ cup grape seed oil

Salt and pepper, to taste

Instructions:

Combine escarole, romaine lettuce, red pepper, red lettuce, green pepper and cherry tomatoes in a large bowl.

Whisk basil, grape seed oil, lemon juice, vinegar, pepper and salt in a bowl. Pour this mixture over the greens and serve immediately.

Pumpkin Cashew Brussels Sprouts Bowl

Ingredients:

16 oz Brussels sprouts, ends trimmed and washed

½ cup cashews

½ cup pumpkin seeds

½ tsp smoked paprika

2 Tbsp Tamari

1 tsp chili powder

1 Tbsp olive oil

1 ½ Tbsp lime juice

¼ cup nutritional yeast

Instructions:

Put Brussels sprouts in a food processor and pulse until loosely chopped.

Add cashews, pumpkin seeds, tamari, chili, smoked paprika, olive oil, lime juice and nutritional yeast then pulse once more until all the ingredients have been well-combined.

You can also do this in the dehydrator by placing the shredded sprouts in the dehydrator sheet and processing overnight.

You may store this dish in an airtight container and it can stay fresh for two weeks.

Always re-heat in the microwave before serving. Enjoy!

Lemon Kale Platter

Ingredients:

12 cups kale, chopped

1 Tbsp minced garlic

2 Tbsp lemon juice

1 tsp soy sauce

1 Tbsp olive oil (add more, as needed)

Salt, to taste

1 tsp soy sauce

Ground black pepper, to taste

Instructions:

Put steamer into a saucepan and fill it with water but make sure that water does not streak past the bottom of the steamer. Boil over high heat before adding Kale then steam for around 5 to 10 minutes or until tender.

Whisk olive oil, soy sauce, garlic, lemon juice, salt and pepper in a bowl. Toss kale in the dressing and make sure that it is well-coated before serving. Enjoy!

Cauliflower Mash and Peas

Ingredients:

1 cup fresh peas, shelled

4 cups cauliflower

4 green onions, sliced thinly

2 tsp cumin

Zest from 1 lemon

A dash of olive oil

1 tsp freshly grated ginger

Arugula

Salt, to taste

Instructions:

From the stem, cut the cauliflower florets and place them in a food processor. Pulse until you get an output that resembles mash.

Add peas and green onions.

In a bowl, whisk lemon zest, lemon juice, cumin and ginger together then pour this over the cauliflower mash. Mix until well-combined.

Serve peas and cauliflower rice on a bed of arugula. Enjoy!

Lettuce and Arugula Salad

Ingredients:

2 cups lettuce, torn

4 cups arugula leaves, rinsed and dried

¼ cup pine nuts

1 cup cherry tomatoes, halved

1 Tbsp rice vinegar

Salt and freshly ground black pepper, to taste

Instructions:

Combine cherry tomatoes, lettuce, arugula, oil, pine nuts and vinegar in a bowl. Season with salt and pepper then cover with a lid. Shake until well-combined.

Serve into plates.

Celery Mushroom Stir-Fry

Ingredients:

1 clove garlic

1 large celeriac, cut into large cubes

2 Tbsp nutritional yeast

Sea salt, to taste

For the Veggie Stir-Fry: 1 bell pepper

4 small carrots, cut into half then sliced

4 celery stalks, sliced

1 cup Crimini mushrooms, sliced

¼ small onion, sliced

For the sauce: 2 Tbsp raw soy sauce

Sesame seeds (for sprinkling)

2 Tbsp cider vinegar

1 Tbsp sesame oil

1 clove garlic, minced

¼ cup raw Tahini

Instructions:

Combine all of the rice ingredients in a food processor and pulse until you get an output that resembles rice. Set the mixture aside.

Mix all of the vegetables in a bowl then whisk the ingredients for the sauce together before pouring it over the vegetables.

Serve the vegetables with garlic rice and with a sprinkling of sesame seeds on top. Enjoy!

Spinach Onion Salad

Ingredients:

1 Tbsp poppy seeds

2 Tbsp sesame seeds

¼ tsp paprika

¼ cup distilled white vinegar

½ cup olive oil

¼ cup almonds, blanched then slivered

10 oz fresh spinach, torn into bite-sized pieces

1 Tbsp onion, minced

¼ tsp Worcestershire sauce

Instructions:

Whisk poppy seeds, sesame seeds, paprika, olive oil, and vinegar in a bowl together with onion and Worcestershire sauce. Chill for around an hour, covered.

Combine spinach and almonds in a large bowl and toss with the greens and the mixture you have made earlier.

Put in the fridge for around 10 to 15 minutes and then serve.

Negative Calorie Diet

Kale and Tomato Stuffed Chicken Breasts

Ingredients:

2 whole free range organic chicken breasts (skinless and boneless), halved

Salt and black pepper, to taste

1 teaspoon poultry seasoning

2 tablespoons of ghee or olive oil

½ cup of fresh kale, minced

¼ cup chopped sun-dried tomatoes

¼ cup of cashew butter

¼ cup of salsa sauce

Directions:

1. Preheat an oven to a temperature of 400°F. Lightly grease a rimmed baking tray with oil and set aside.

2. Add ½ cup of water into a pan, apply medium-high heat and bring to a boil. Add the kale, dried tomatoes and ½ tablespoon of oil and cook until the kale is wilted

and the tomatoes have softened. Season to taste with salt and pepper and remove the pan from heat.

3. Flattened the halved chicken breast with a meat mallet and season both sides with salt, pepper and poultry seasoning. Divide the kale-tomato mixture and cashew butter on four chicken breasts, roll it up and secure the end with toothpick.

4. Lightly brush the outer part with oil and transfer into the greased baking tray. Bake for about 25 minutes or until lightly golden and cooked through.

5. Remove from the oven, let it rest for 5 minutes and cut into halves or thin slices.

6. Transfer to a serving plate and serve warm with tomato salsa.

Salmon, Avocado and Cucumber Green Salad

Ingredients:

1 fillet wild Atlantic salmon, skinless

¼ teaspoon garlic powder

¼ teaspoon Italian seasoning

Salt and black pepper, to taste

1 lime, juiced

2 teaspoons grass fed ghee

2 cups loosely packed fresh kale, cut into chiffonade

1 ripe avocado, cubed

1 small cucumber, sliced into rounds

2 tablespoons minced parsley

For the Dressing:

2 tablespoons of olive oil

1 lime, juiced

Salt and pepper

1 tablespoon minced dill

Directions:

1. Season the salmon with salt, pepper, garlic powder and Italian seasoning and drizzle with lime juice on both sides.

2. Add the ghee in a skillet over medium-high heat and fry the salmon for about 3 minutes on each side. Remove from skillet, let it rest for 5 minutes on a plate and cut into cubes.

3. Whisk all dressing ingredients in a large bowl, add in the rest of the ingredients and gently toss to evenly coat the salad ingredients with dressing.

4. Divide into four serving bowls, top with salmon and serve immediately.

Lemon Pepper Kale and Garlic Salmon

Ingredients:

1 salmon fillet

Half a bunch of fresh kale, chopped

1 red bell pepper, sliced

5 cloves of garlic, finely chopped

Juice from one medium sized freshly squeezed lemon

1-2 tablespoons of almond butter

Half a red onion, diced

3 tablespoons of lemon pepper (or to taste)

Directions:

1. In a non-stick pan, or a pan lightly coated extra virgin olive oil, fry the salmon fillet 3-5 minutes per side over medium heat.

2. With one minute left of cooking, add half the finely chopped garlic and lemon juice to the pan, then spoon over salmon fillet when serving.

3. Melt the almond butter in a pan over medium-low heat and add onion and red bell pepper.

4. After 3 minutes, add the chopped kale and the other half of the garlic. Sprinkle with lemon pepper.

5. Use tongs to turn and mix the kale with the other ingredients in the pan. Ensure the kale is heated evenly. Remove after only 2 minutes.

6. Serve and enjoy! For more lemon flavor, garnish the salmon fillet with a thin slice of lemon and sprinkle with lemon pepper.

Toasty Kale Pecan Squash

Ingredients:

1 medium sized butternut squash

3 garlic cloves, minced

4 tablespoons fresh parsley, chopped

Pinch of ground course sea salt (or to taste)

Half a tablespoon of extra virgin olive oil

1 cup of fresh chopped kale

ADDITIONAL INGREDIENTS TO BE PROCESSED:

1 tablespoon of nutritional yeast

0.25 cups of almonds

0.25 cups of pecans

1 teaspoon of extra virgin olive oil

Pinch of ground course sea salt

Directions:

1. Preheat oven to 400F and lightly coat your casserole dish with oil.

2. Peel the squash, remove the top and bottom, then cut into two halves. Scoop out the guts and seeds. Further chop the two halves of squash into cubes of about 3 cm each and add the cubes to the casserole dish.

3. Add parsley, salt, minced garlic, and oil into the casserole dish and stir until well mixed with the squash cubes.

4. Cover and bake for 40-50 minutes.

5. While baking, combine the pecans, almonds, yeast, as well as a pinch of salt and 1 teaspoon of extra virgin olive oil in your food processor until chunky. Do not puree.

6. After 40-50 minutes, remove squash from the oven and turn off the heat. Add the chopped kale and sprinkle the mixture from the food processor all over the squash. Then return to the still hot oven for 5 minutes to warm the processed ingredients. Serve and enjoy!

Tomato Garlic Kale Salad

Ingredients:

Five sun-dried tomatoes

A handful of finely chopped kale

A handful of finely chopped spinach

1 Tbsp pumpkin seeds

¼ small, red onion

One garlic clove

For the dressing:

1 tsp apple cider vinegar

1 Tbsp cold pressed oil

A dash of garlic powder, pepper and chili

¼ tsp salt

For the toppings:

fresh herbs and cherry tomatoes

Directions:

1. Place spinach and kale in a bowl and mix the dressing ingredients in another bowl.

2. Pour the dressing over the greens then chop the tomatoes, red onion and garlic clove. Add them to the greens and sprinkle pumpkin seeds on top.

3. Mix until well-combined and serve topped with cherry tomatoes and fresh herbs.

Mushroom and Spinach Frittata

Ingredients:

1 tablespoon ghee

½ cup of sliced button mushrooms

¼ cup minced shallot

2 cups loosely packed baby spinach

6 free range organic eggs

¼ almond milk

Salt and pepper, to taste

½ teaspoon mixed Italian herbs

1 tomato, sliced into rounds

1 cup of precooked free range chicken breast, diced

Directions:

1. Add the ghee in a skillet and apply medium-high heat. Sauté the shallot, mushroom and spinach for 5 minutes.

2. While sautéing the vegetables, whisk the eggs, milk, Italian herbs, a pinch of salt and pepper in a bowl and

pour it into the skillet. Top with diced chicken and tomatoes, cover skillet and reduce heat to low.

3. Cook for about 10 minutes, or until the eggs are set and the bottom is lightly brown. Remove the skillet from heat and let it stand for 5 minutes with cover.

4. Slide the frittata on a serving plate, slice into 4 wedges and serve warm.

Kale and Quinoa Salad

Ingredients:

1 cup quinoa

2 cups water

2 Tbsp lemon juice

3 Tbsp olive oil

10 leaves kale, cut into small pieces

1 tsp Dijon mustard

1 cup currants

1 cup pecans

½ tsp ground sea salt

1 tsp freshly cracked black pepper

1 large garlic clove, minced

Instructions:

In a saucepan, boil water with quinoa. After boiling, reduce the heat to low and cook for around 12 minutes or until quinoa has absorbed the water. Let the mixture rest for around 5 minutes then allow quinoa to cool completely and then put the kale in a large bowl.

Whisk Dijon mustard, olive oil, pepper, lemon juice, garlic and salt in a bowl altogether until oil has emulsified. Use this mixture as a dressing for the salad and drizzle it over the kale leaves.

Add pecans, quinoa, and currants to the kale leaves and toss until well-combined.

Serve and enjoy!

Chapter 8: Negative Calorie Diet Soup Recipes

Onion and Cilantro Soup

Ingredients:

½ cup water

1 ½ cups shelled edamame, frozen then thawed before steaming

1 Tbsp fresh cilantro, chopped

¼ cup white onion, chopped

1 can cannellini beans, drained

2 tsp chili powder

½ tsp salt

2 Tbsp balsamic vinegar

Instructions:

Mix all of the ingredients in a food processor and puree until creamy and well-blended.

Serve and enjoy! You may also serve this with a cup of vegetables if desired.

Tomato Carrot Lentil Soup

Ingredients:

2 carrots, diced

¼ cup olive oil

1 onion, chopped

1 bay leaf

1 tsp dried oregano

2 cloves garlic, minced

2 stalks celery, chopped

1 tsp dried basil

2 Tbsp vinegar

½ cup spinach, rinsed and sliced thinly

8 cups water

2 cups dry lentils

1 can tomatoes, crushed

Instructions:

Heat oil in a large pot over medium heat then add celery, carrots and onions. Add onion and cook until tender then add bay leaf, garlic, basil and oregano and cook for 2 minutes more.

Add water, lentils and tomatoes and boil the mixture. Simmer after reducing the heat for at least an hour.

After simmering, add spinach and cook until spinach is wilted and then add vinegar and season with salt and pepper, to taste.

Serve with extra vinegar, if desired. Enjoy!

Zucchini Spinach Soup

Ingredients:

2 plum tomatoes, chopped

1/8 tsp salt

1 small zucchini, diced finely

1 large shallot, chopped finely

1 can reduced sodium chicken broth

1 ½ cups baby spinach, packed

½ tsp Italian Seasoning

Instructions:

Add Italian seasoning, zucchini and shallot to a pan heated over low-medium heat and cook for around 2 to 3 minutes or until vegetables are soft. Add broth, increase heat and bring the mixture to a boil. Make sure to stir occasionally then reduce heat and simmer.

Add spinach and cook for around 2 minutes.

Serve and enjoy!

Celery Carrot Basil Soup

Ingredients:

1 large onion, diced

1 large carrot, diced

2 stalks celery, diced

4 cloves garlic, minced

1 tsp dried oregano

1/3 lb green beans, cut into 1 ½ inch pieces

1 tsp dried basil

1 can unsalted diced tomatoes

Kosher salt

Freshly ground pepper

6 cups low sodium chicken broth

2 Tbsp fresh basil, chopped

Instructions:

In a large pot heat onions on medium heat for 2 minutes then add the garlic and cook for 30 seconds more. Add carrot and celery and cook for around 5 minutes or until they are soft. Add dried oregano, green beans, ¾ teaspoon salt, basil and cook for 3 minutes. Season with salt and pepper, to taste.

Next, add the chicken broth and tomatoes and bring mixture to a boil. After boiling, reduce the heat to low and simmer for 10 more minutes.

Pour into bowls and season with salt, to taste.

Garnish with chopped basil. Enjoy!

Red Lentil Soup

Ingredients:

1 cup red lentils, washed thoroughly

3 celery stalks, chopped

1 large onion, chopped

2 large carrots, chopped

2 tablespoons of tomato paste

2 cups of broccoli florets

Pinch of oregano

1 bay leaf

6 leaves of basil, chopped

Pinch of ground thyme

5 cups water

Directions:

1. Simply combine ingredients in a slow cooker and cook for 4-5 hours on high.

Negative Calorie Diet

Delicious Cauliflower and Celery Fat Loss Soup

Ingredients:

1 large cauliflower (between 2 and 3 pounds)

3 medium onions, chopped

3 celery stalks, chopped

1 teaspoon of paprika

1 teaspoon of onion powder

1 teaspoon of garlic powder

2 tablespoons of coconut oil

1 tablespoon of white wine vinegar

5 cups of water

1 bay leaf

2 garlic cloves, minced

1 tablespoon of freshly squeezed lime juice

Ground course sea salt according to taste

Directions:

1. Heat a medium sized dutch oven and pour in the coconut oil, then add onions and celery and cook for 3 minutes, then add garlic and cook for an additional one minute.

2. Add the vinegar and stir until it evaporates.

3. Stir in all the spices

4. Add the chopped cauliflower, salt, bay leaf, and water. Heat until it boils

5. Lower heat, cover, and simmer.

6. When the cauliflower is soft, remove bay leaf and stir to make the soup's texture more creamy, then serve

Chapter 9: Negative Calorie Diet Juice Recipes

For each of the juice recipes below, the directions are the same and so they are not repeated at the outset of each recipe. Simply clean your produce and insert into your juicer. The juice is best consumed immediately but can be stored for up to 12 hours.

Kale-aid

One large cucumber

Six leaves of kale

Two medium sized apples

Two cups of spinach

One lemon

Kale is considered a "super food" and is ideal for weight loss due to its high concentration of nutrients and low calorie content. It is among the most nutrient-dense vegetables available and this juice makes sure you can easily consume this amazing vegetable daily. Kale is also a significant source of organo-sulfur compounds. Studies show these compounds are effective at fighting many different types of cancer.

Kale Power

Five leaves of kale

One cup of collard greens

One medium sized red bell pepper

One medium sized apple (any variety you like)

Two handfuls of cilantro

Five medium sized carrots

In addition to promoting overall bodily health, this juice can be an effective cancer deterrent. The collard greens are rich in nutrients that have powerful cancer fighting properties. Studies have shown both kale and collard greens can be beneficial at fighting and preventing breast cancer, prostate cancer, colon cancer, and other cancers.

Just Kale Me Now!

Four leaves of kale

Two large stalks of celery

One small cucumber (or half of one medium sized cucumber)

One medium sized pear, any variety

Half of one lime

One cup of spinach

Kale is such a healthy vegetable that you'll want to consume it as often as possible. You can cycle through the various kale recipes in this book to keep yourself from getting bored. Juices with significant kale quantity and little to no fruit, like this juice, are excellent juices for weight loss. This is because kale is extremely nutrient dense. Drinking kale juice means that you can easily get an entire day's supply of many vitamins and nutrients while hardly consuming any calories.

Green Stacks

Two cups of spinach

One handful of parsley

Two medium sized Granny Smith apples

Three leaves of kale

The apples provide a hint of sweetness that will make this drink a favorite even for people who dislike the taste of kale and spinach. The parsley in this juice will also help to reduce the gas and bloating that some people experience when juicing with raw kale. The spinach is a great intestinal tract cleanser that reduces the buildup of waste and facilitates the body's digestive system working efficiently without any digestive issues.

Green Cleanse

Five large stalks of celery

Two medium sized Granny Smith apples

One medium sized cucumber

Two handfuls of spinach

Five leaves of kale

One quarter of a lemon, peeled

One half of a lime, peeled

This juice is a solid choice for anyone wanting to focus on cleansing the body of toxins. Cleansing can be an effective way to jump start a recovery after a binge on unhealthy food or toxic substances like alcohol. It can also be a great way to energize the body even when you normally eat well and live an active lifestyle.

Apple of my Eye

Four medium sized apples
One English cucumber
Two stalks of celery
One large orange, peeled
One thumbnail sized piece of ginger root

A tasty apple juice with a ginger kick! The celery, although perhaps not the tastiest produce, is high in vitamins and minerals that help to maintain the skin's youthful elasticity and aid complexion. Celery can also help to calm the nerves and reduce high blood pressure. The orange juice also helps to protect the skin by attacking and eliminating free radicals within the body

Guava and Green

Two medium sized guava, or one large guava (peeled or unpeeled according to preference)
One medium sized Granny Smith apple
One large cucumber
Two stalks of celery
One kiwi

Guava is a delicious "super fruit" widely consumed in some tropical countries. It earned its reputation as a super fruit due to its high concentration of a wide variety of nutrients and its many health benefits. Among other vitamins, minerals, and nutrients, Guava is particularly rich in copper, vitamin C, lycopene, and antioxidants.

Conclusion

Ultimately, improving your health, losing weight, and living an amazing life are all within your grasp. Let the negative calorie diet be your tool for achieving these goals. With what you have learned in this book and the many delicious negative calorie recipes you now have at your disposal you have everything you need to succeed.

Join Albert Pino's VIP Club

Get access to exclusive content from Albert including healthy living tips, tricks and hacks, special discounts, recipes, and free books!

www.albertpino.com

Made in the USA
Las Vegas, NV
12 April 2023

70501585R00056